From Snorri Sturluson's Edda

THE VIKING GODS

Illustrated by Lorenz Frölich
Watercoloured by Eggert Pétursson

From Snorri Sturluson's Edda

THE
VIKING
GODS

Translated from the original 13th-century text
by Jean I. Young PhD

Edited by Jon Thorisson

Illustrations by Lorenz Frölich
Watercoloured by Eggert Pétursson

Translation by jean I. Young MA, PhD
Late Senior Lecturer in English at the University of Reading.
First published in 1954 by Bowes & Bowes Publishers Limited, Cambridge, England under the title: "The Prose Edda of Snorri Sturluson: Tales from Norse Mythology."
This edition is a revised and abbreviated version of the original translation.
Published with kind permission from the Jean I. Young estate.

Introduction adapted from: "The Younger Edda: also called Snorri's Edda or The Prose Edda," translated by Rasmus B. Anderson, former Professor of Scandinavian Languages at the University of Wisconsin. Published by S. C. Griggs and Company, Chicago, U.S.A and Trübner & Co., London, England 1880.

Lorenz Frölich text © Hanne Westergaard. Former curator, Department of Painting and Sculpture, The Royal Museum of Fine Arts, Copenhagen.

Snorri. Story-teller of the Gods © Páll Valsson, Senior Lecturer in Icelandic, University of Uppsala, Sweden

Illustrations on inside covers first published in Finn Magnussen's "Oldnordisk Verdensbetragtning," Copenhagen 1824-26.

Illustrations on pages 8, 17, 21, 24, 30, 32, 38, 42, 44, 46, 50, 52 and 54 by Lorenz Frölich, first published in "Den Ældre Eddas Gudesange," Copenhagen 1895

All other illustrations are from Lorenz Frölich's "Nordens Guder," a limited edition of graphic prints, Copenhagen 1873-1887, published with permission from The Royal Museum of Fine Arts, Copenhagen, Denmark.
Photography by Hans Petersen

Illustrations watercoloured by Eggert Pétursson

Edited by Jon Thorisson
Cover design and layout: Jon Thorisson and Helgi Hilmarsson

© Gudrun publishing 1995
Reykjavík – www.gudrunpublishing.com

1. impression 1995
2. impression 1996
3. impression 1997
4. impression 1999
5. impression 2001
6. impression 2003
7. impression 2006, New edition

Published with the support of the Nordic Cultural Fund

ISBN 9979-856-90-4 (Hard cover)
ISBN 9979-856-78-5 (Paperback)

Berkeley 6-24p and Goudy 14p

Printed in India

Contents

III. *The Golden Age*

IV. *Divine Treasures*

Appendix

Editor's Note

This book contains excerpts from Snorri Sturluson's Edda, written in the thirteenth century.

For the sake of readability, this book is divided into short chapters. In each episode, Snorri presents a sharp and entertaining picture of the world as the Vikings saw it, and of the gods that they worshipped and sought inspiration from.

The main aim of this edition is to give readers some insight into the ideas and imaginations of people in the past – a cosmogony that no one has portrayed with greater artistry and narrative skill than Snorri Sturluson.

His inspired account of the creation of the world, of the family of gods and their life in Asgard and Valhalla, is written with deep understanding of human nature and filled with warm humour.

The Edda has been called "one of the great story-books of the Middle Ages."

Many people have assisted with this publication. Above all, thanks are due to the Jean I. Young estate for their kind permission to use her outstanding translation. The staff of the Royal Museum of Fine Arts in Copenhagen provided invaluable help with collecting illustrations. Art historian Hanne Westergaard wrote the text on Lorenz Frölich. Páll Valsson, lecturer at the University of Uppsala in Sweden, wrote the chapter on Snorri Sturluson. Bernard Scudder translated two verses from "The Sibyl's Vision" (Völuspá) for the chapter The Creation of Man, and read the first proof; Don Brandt read the second proof.

My warmest thanks to all these people for their kind assistance.

Jon Thorisson

Introduction

Chaos

In the beginning, before the heaven and the earth and the sea were created, the great abyss Ginnungagap was without form and void, and the spirit of Fimbultyr moved upon the face of the deep, until the ice-cold rivers, flowing from Niflheim, came in contact with the dazzling flames from Muspell. This was before Chaos.

And Fimbultyr said: Let the melted drops of vapour quicken into life, and the giant Ymir was born in the midst of Ginnungagap. He was not a god, but the father of all the race of evil giants. This was Chaos.

Cosmos

And Fimbultyr said: Let Ymir be slain and let order be established. And straightaway Odin and his brothers – the bright sons of Buri – gave Ymir a mortal wound, and from his body they made the universe; from his flesh, the earth; from his blood, the sea; from his bones, the rocks; from his hair, the trees; from his skull, the vaulted heavens; from his eyebrows, the stronghold called Midgard. And the gods formed man and woman in their own image of two trees, and breathed into them the breath of life. Ask and Embla became living souls, and they received a garden in Midgard as a dwelling-place for themselves and their children until the end of time.

This was Cosmos.

The Family of Gods

The gods themselves dwelt in Asgard. Some of them were of the mighty Æsir-race: All-father Odin, and Frigg his Queen; Thor, the master of Mjölnir; Baldur, the good; the one-handed Tyr; Bragi, the song-smith; Idun with the youth-giving apples, and Heimdall, the watcher of Asgard. Others were mild and gentle Vanir: Njörd, Frey, and Freyja, the goddess of love; but in the midst of Asgard in daily con-

10

tact with the gods, the serpent Loki, the friend of the giants, winded on his slimy coils.

To these gods the Vikings offered sacrifices, to them prayers ascended, and from them came such blessings as each god found it proper to bestow.

Life in Asgard

Most of all these gods were worshipped on the battle-field, for there was the home of the Viking. There he lived and there he hoped some day to die; for if the Norns, the weavers of fate, permitted him to fall sword in hand, then he would not descend to the shades of Hel, but be carried in Valkyrian arms up to Valhalla, where a new life would be granted unto him, or better, where he would continue his earthly life in contact with the gods.

Happy gatherings at the banquet, where the flowing mead-horn was passed freely round, and where words of wisdom and wit abounded, or martial games with sharp swords and spears, were the delight of the Æsir. Under the ash Yggdrasill they met in council, and if they ever appeared outside of the walls of Asgard, it was to go on errands of love, or to make war on the giants, their enemies from the beginning.

Thus lived the gods in heaven very much like their worshippers on earth, except that Idun's apples preserved them ever fresh and youthful.

Innocence Departs

But Loki, the serpent, was in the midst of them. Frigg's heart was filled with gloomy forebodings in regard to Baldur, her beloved son, and her mind could not find rest until all things that could harm him had sworn not to injure Baldur. Now they had nothing to fear for the best god, and with perfect abandon and security they amused themselves by making him serve as a mark, and hurled darts, stones and other weapons at him, whom nothing could scathe. But the serpent Loki was more subtle than any one within or without Asgard, whom Fimbultyr had made; and he came to Höd, the blind god, put the tender mistletoe in his hand and directed his arm, so that Baldur sank from the joys of Valhalla down into the abodes of pale Hel, and did not return. Loki is bound and tortured, but innocence has

11

departed from Asgard; among men there are bloody wars; brothers slay brothers; sensual sins grow huge; perjury has taken the place of truth. The elements themselves become discordant, and then comes the great Fimbul-winter, with its howling storms and terrible snow, that darkens the air and takes all gladness from the sun.

Ragnarök

The world's last day approaches. All bonds and fetters that bound the forces of heaven and earth together are severed, and the powers of good and evil are brought together in an internecine feud. Loki advances with the Fenriswolf and the Midgard Serpent, his own children, with all the hosts of the giants, and with Surt, who flings fire and flame over the world. Odin advances with all the gods and his Champions. They meet, contend, and fall. The wolf swallows Odin, but Vidar, the Silent, sets his foot upon the monster's lower jaw, he seizes the other with his hand, and thus rends him till he dies. Frey encounters Surt, and terrible blows are given before Frey falls. Heimdall and Loki fight and kill each other, and so do Tyr and the dog Garm from the Gnipa Cave. Thor fells the Midgard Serpent with his hammer Mjölnir, but he retreats only nine paces when he himself falls dead, suffocated by the serpent's venom. Then smoke wreathes up around the ash Yggdrasill, the high flames play against the heavens, the graves of the gods, of the giants and of men are swallowed up by the sea, and the end has come. This is Ragnarök, the doom of the gods.

The Earth Rises Again

But the radiant dawn follows the night. The earth, completely green, rises again from the sea, and where the gulls have but been rocking on restless waves, rich fields unplowed and unsown now wave their golden harvests before the gentle breezes. The gods awake to a new life, Baldur is with them again. Then comes the mighty Fimbultyr, the god who is from everlasting to everlasting; the god whom the Edda skald dared not name. The god of gods comes to the Æsir. He comes to the great judgement and gathers all the good into Gimli to dwell there forever, and evermore delights enjoy; but the perjurers and murder-

12

ers and adulterers he sends to Nastrand, that terrible hall, to be torn until they are purged from their wickedness. This is Regeneration.

These are the outlines of the Viking religion. Such were the doctrines established by Odin among man. Thus do we find it recorded in the Eddas of Iceland.

Sons and Daughters of Odin

We send this book into the world with the hope that it may aid some young son or daughter of Odin to find his way to the fountains of Urd and Mimir and to Idun's rejuvenating apples. The son must not squander, but husband wisely, what his father has accumulated. Man must cherish and hold fast and add to the thought that the past has bequeathed to him. Thus does it grow greater and richer with each new generation. The past is the mirror that reflects the future.

I. The Beginning

The First World

In the beginning
not anything existed,
there was no sand nor sea
nor cooling waves;
earth was unknown
and heaven above
only Ginnungagap
was – there was no grass.

The first world to exist was Muspell in the
southern hemisphere; it is light and hot and that
region flames and burns so that those who do
not belong to it and whose native land it is not,
cannot endure it. The one who sits there at
land's end to guard it is called Surt; he has a
flaming sword, and at the end of the world he
will come and harry and will vanquish all the
gods and burn the whole world with fire. – As it
says in the Sibyl's Vision:

Surt from the south comes
with spoiler of twigs
blazing his sword
like sun of the Mighty Ones:
mountains will crash down,
troll-women stumble,
men tread the road to Hel,
heaven's rent asunder.

That part of Ginnungagap which turned
northwards became full of the ice and the

sparkling frost's weight and heaviness, and within there was drizzling rain and gusts of wind.
But the southern part of Ginnungagap became
light by meeting the sparks and glowing embers
which flew out of the world of Muspell.

Just as cold and all harsh things emanated
from Niflheim, so everything in the neighbour-
hood of Muspell was warm and bright.
Ginnungagap was as mild as windless air, and
where the soft air of the heat met the frost so
that it thawed and dripped, then, by the might
of that which sent the heat, life appeared in the
drops of running fluid and grew into the like-
ness of a man. He was given the name Ymir.

The Frost Ogres

Ymir and all his family were evil; we call them frost ogres. But it is said that while he slept he fell into a sweat; then there grew under his left arm a man and woman, and one of his legs got a son with the other, and that is where the families of frost ogres come from.

As soon as the frost thawed, it became a cow called Audhumla, and four rivers of milk ran from her teats, and she fed Ymir.

She licked the ice-blocks which were salty, and by the evening of the first day of the block-licking appeared a man's hair, on the second day a man's head, and on the third day the whole man was there. He was called Buri. He was handsome and tall and strong. He had a son called Bor, who married a woman called Bestla.

They had three sons; the first, Odin; the second, Vili; the third, Ve; and it is my belief that Odin, in association with his brothers, is the ruler of heaven and earth. We think that that is his title; it is the name given to the man we know to be greatest and most famous.

The Creation of Heaven and Earth

Bor's sons killed the giant Ymir and carried him into the middle of Ginnungagap, and made the world from him: from his blood the sea and lakes, from his flesh the earth, from his bones the mountains; rocks and pebbles they made from his teeth and jaws and those bones that were broken.

From the blood which welled freely from his wounds they fashioned the ocean, when they put together the earth and girdled it, laying the ocean round about it. To cross it would strike most men as impossible.

They also took his skull and made the sky from it and set it over the earth with its four sides, and under each corner they put a dwarf. These are called: East, West, North, and South. Then they took the sparks and burning embers that were flying about after they had been blown out of Muspell, and placed them in the midst of Ginnungagap to give light to heaven above and earth beneath.

They gave their stations to all the stars, some fixed in the sky; others that had wandered at will in the firmament were now given their appointed places and the paths in which they were to travel. So it is said in ancient poems that from that time sprang the reckoning of days and years.

The earth is round, and surrounding it lies the deep sea, and on the strand of that sea they gave lands to the families of giants to settle, but inland Bor's sons built a stronghold round the world on account of the hostility of the giants; for this stronghold they used Ymir's eyebrows, and they called it Midgard. They took his brains too and flung them up into the air and made from them the clouds.

The Creation of Man

When they were going along the sea-shore, the
sons of Bor found two trees and they picked
these up and created men from them. The first
gave them spirit and life; the second, understanding and power of movement; the third,
form, speech, hearing and sight. They gave them
clothes and names.

The man was called Ask and the woman
Embla; and from them have sprung the races of
men who were given Midgard to live in.

Until three mighty
and beloved gods
from that band
approached.
On the shore they found
Ask and Embla,
capable of little,
their destiny unformed.

They had no spirit,
they had no sense,
neither blood nor voice
nor fine complexion.
Odin gave them spirit,
Hænir gave them voice,
Lod gave them blood
and fine complexion.

II. The Family of Gods

Odin and Frigg

The foremost or oldest of all the gods is called All-father in our tongue, but in ancient Asgard he had twelve names.

He lives for ever and ever, and rules over the whole of his kingdom and governs all things great and small.

He created heaven and earth and the sky and all that in them is.

His greatest achievement, however, is the making of man and giving him a soul which will live and never die, although his body may decay to dust or burn to ashes. All righteous men shall live and be with him where it is called Gimli or Vingolf but wicked men will go to Hel and thence to Niflheim that is down in the ninth world.

His wife, the daughter of Fjörgvin, was named Frigg, and from that family has come the kindred that inhabited ancient Asgard and those kingdoms belonging to it; we call the members of that family the Æsir and they are all divinities.

Odin is called All-father because he is the father of all the gods. He is also called Valfather (Father-of-the-slain) because all who fall in battle are his adopted sons. He allots to them Valhalla and Vingolf, and then they are called Champions.

Thor and Sif

Thor is son of Odin, husband of Sif. I do not know Sif's genealogy but she was a most beautiful woman with hair like gold. Thor rules over that kingdom called Thrudvangar and his hall is called Bilskirnir; in that building are six hundred and forty floors – it is the largest house known to men. As Odin says in the Lay of Grimnir:

> Bilskirnir with its winding ways
> I know has more
> than six hundred and forty floors,
> of those buildings
> I know to be roofed
> I know my son's is the largest.

Thor has two goats and the chariot he drives in. The goats pull the chariot, and for this reason he is called Thor-the-charioteer.

He also owns three precious things. One is the hammer Mjölnir which the frost ogres and cliff giants know when it is raised aloft, and that is not surprising since he has cracked the skulls of many of their kith and kin. His second great treasure is a belt of strength, and when he buckles that on his divine might is doubled. And he owns a third thing of great value in his iron gauntlets; he cannot do without these when he grips the handle of the hammer.

But no one is well-informed enough to be able to recount all his mighty deeds.

Baldur and Nanna

Baldur is son of Odin and Frigg, husband of Nanna, owner of Hringhorni and Draupnir. God of lamentations.

There is nothing but good to be told of him. He is the best of them and everyone sings his praises. He is so fair of face and bright that a splendour radiates from him, and there is one flower so white that it is likened to Baldur's brow; it is the whitest of all flowers. From that you can tell how beautiful his body is, and how bright his hair.

He is the wisest of the gods, and the sweetest spoken, and the most merciful, but it is a characteristic of his that none of his decisions can be fulfilled. He lives in the place in heaven called Breidablik; nothing impure can be there, as it says here:

There where Baldur
has built his dwellings
they call it Breidablik;
in that land
where I know
there are fewest evil things.

Njörd and Skadi

The third god is the one called Njörd. He lives in heaven at a place called Noatun. He controls the path of the wind, stills sea and fire, and is to be invoked for seafaring and fishing.

Njörd has a wife called Skadi, daughter of the giant Thjazi. Skadi wanted to have the homestead her father had had, on some mountains in the place called Thrymheim, but Njörd wanted to be near the sea. They came to an agreement that they should be nine nights in Thrymheim and then another nine at Noatun. When Njörd came back to Noatun from the mountain, however, he said this:

> Mountains I loathed,
> no longer than nine
> nights did I stay there,
> the howling of wolves
> seemed ugly to me
> compared with the whooping of swans.

Then Skadi said this:

> I could not sleep
> by the shore of the sea
> for the noise of the mew
> that awakened me,
> the bird that flew
> each dawn from the deep.

Then Skadi went up the mountain and lived in Thrymheim, and she goes about a great deal on skis and with her bow and arrow shoots wild animals.

Frey
The Harvest God

Njörd of Noatun had two children after this, a son called Frey and a daughter Freyja. They were beautiful to look at, and powerful.

Frey is an exceedingly famous god; he decides when the sun shall shine or the rain come down, and along with that the fruitfulness of the earth, and he is good to invoke for peace and plenty. He also brings about the prosperity of men.

Some dwarfs, the sons of Ivaldi, made Skid-bladnir and gave the ship to Frey. It is so big that all the Æsir with weapons and armour can find room in it and, wherever it is going, a breeze springs up as soon as its sail is hoisted. Moreover, it is made of so many things and with such cunning that when it has not to go to sea, it can be folded together like a cloth and kept in one's pouch.

Skidbladnir is a fine ship, and mighty magic will have been used to get it made like this.

Freyja
The Goddess of Love

Freyja is the most renowned of the goddesses. She owns that homestead in heaven known as Folkvangar and whenever she rides into battle she has half the slain and Odin half, as it says here:

> Folkvangar's where
> Freyja decides
> who shall sit where in the hall;
> half the slain every day
> she chooses
> and Odin half.

Her hall Sessrumnir is large and beautiful. When she goes on a journey she sits in a chariot drawn by two cats. She is most readily invoked, and from her name derives the polite custom of calling the wives of men of rank Fru. She enjoys love poetry, and it is good to call on her for help in love affairs.

Freyja is as distinguished as Frigg. She is married to a man called Od. Od went away on long journeys and Freyja weeps for him, and her tears are red gold. Freyja has many names, and the reason for this is that she gave herself several when she went to look for Od among peoples she did not know. Freyja owns the necklace of the Brisings. She is also called the divinity of the Vanir.

Tyr
The Battle God

There is a god called Tyr. He is the boldest and most courageous, and has power over victory in battle; it is good for brave men to invoke him. It is a proverbial saying that he who surpasses others and does not waver is "Tyr-valiant." He is also so well informed that a very knowledgeable man is said to be "Tyr-wise".

Here is one proof of his daring. When the gods tried to persuade the wolf Fenrir to allow the fetter Gleipnir to be placed on him, he did not believe that they would free him until they put Tyr's hand in his mouth as a pledge. Then, when the Æsir would not loose him, he bit off the hand.

So Tyr is one-handed and he is not called a peace-maker.

Bragi and Idun

One god is called Bragi. He is famous for wisdom and most of all for eloquence and skill with words; he knows most about poetry and from him poetry gets its name.

The beginning of poetry was that the gods were at war with the people known as the Vanir and they arranged for a peace-meeting between them and made a truce in this way: they both went up to a crock and spat into it. When they were going away, the gods took the truce token and would not allow it to be lost, and made of it a man. He was called Kvasir. He is so wise that nobody asks him any question he is unable to answer. He travelled far and wide over the world to teach men wisdom and came once to feast with some dwarfs. These called him aside for a word in private and killed him, letting his blood run into two crocks and one kettle. They mixed his blood with honey, and it became the mead which makes whoever drinks of it a poet or scholar.

Odin gave the mead to the Æsir and those men who can compose poetry.

Bragi's wife is Idun. She keeps in her box the apples the gods have to eat, when they grow old, to become young again, and so it will continue up to Ragnarök.

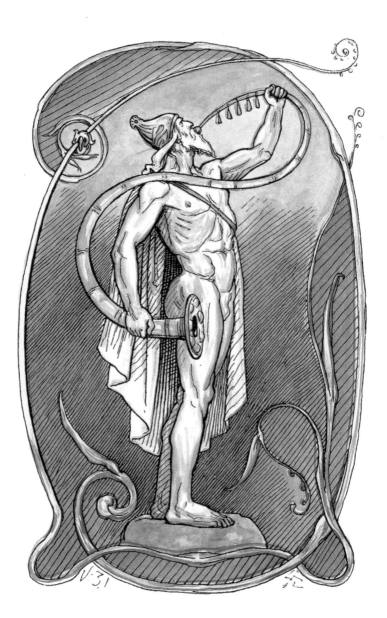

Heimdall
Warden of the Gods

"Of nine mothers I'm the son
and son of nine sisters too."

One is called Heimdall. He is called the white
god, and he is great and holy. Nine maidens
gave birth to him, and all of them sisters. He is
also known as Goldtooth, he had teeth of gold.
His horse is called Goldtuft. He lives in a place
called Himinbjörg by Bifröst. He is warden of
the gods, and sits there at the end of heaven to
guard the bridge from the cliff giants. He needs
less sleep than a bird, and can see a hundred
leagues in front of him as well by night as by
day. He can hear the grass growing on the earth
and the wool on sheep, and everything that
makes more noise. He has the trumpet known
as the horn Gjöll, and its blast can be heard over
all the worlds. A name for a head is Heimdall's
sword. So it is said:

Himinbjörg's said to be
the name of Heimdall's house;
there the warden of the gods
glad
in his gracious home
drinks the good mead.

The Blind, the Bold and the Beautiful

Höd is one of the gods. He is blind. He is immensely strong too, but the gods would rather there were no need to mention his name, since his handiwork will long be remembered amongst gods and men.

Vidar is the name of one of them, the silent god. He has a stout shoe and is almost as strong as Thor. The gods rely greatly on him in all difficult situations.

Vali is the name of one, a son of Odin and Rind; he is bold in battle and a very good shot.

Ull, Sif's son and Thor's stepson, is one too. He is such a good archer and ski-runner that no one can rival him. He is beautiful to look at as well and he has all the characteristics of a warrior. It is also good to call on him in duels.

Forseti is the son of Baldur and Nanna. He owns the large hall in heaven known as Glitnir. Without exception all who come to him with legal disputes go away reconciled; that is the best court known to gods and men.

Loki
The Father of Lies

Also reckoned amongst the gods is one that some call the mischiefmonger of the Æsir and the father-of-lies and the disgrace-of-gods-and-men. He is the son of the giant Farbauti and his name is Loki. Loki is handsome and fair of face, but has an evil disposition and is very changeable of mood.

He excelled all men in the art of cunning, and he always cheats. He was continually involving the Æsir in great difficulties and he often helped them out again by guile. His wife's name is Sigyn; their son is Narvi.

Loki had still more children. There was a giantess in Giantland called Angurboda. Loki had three children by her, the first was the wolf Fenrir, the second is the Midgard Serpent – and the third Hel. Now when the gods knew that these three children were being brought up in Giantland and had gathered from prophecy that they would meet with great harm and misfortune on their account, All-father sent some of the gods to capture the children and bring them to him. And when they came to him, he flung the serpent into the deep sea which surrounds the whole world. He threw Hel into Niflheim and gave her authority over nine worlds.

The gods brought the wolf up at home, and only Tyr had the courage to go up to it and give it food.

III. The Golden Age

VErs.5.

Asgard
A Divine City

The gods built a stronghold for themselves in
the middle of the world, which is called Asgard.
There the gods and their kindred lived, and
from then on came to pass many events and
memorable happenings both in heaven and
earth. There is a place there called Hlidskjalf,
and when Odin sat there on his high seat he saw
over the whole world and what everyone was
doing, and he understood everything he saw.

Once Asgard was built Odin appointed rulers who, along with him, were to control the destinies of men, and decide how the stronghold should be governed. That was in the place called Idavöll in the middle of the stronghold. Their first task was to build a temple in which there were seats for the twelve of them, apart from the high seat of the All-father. That is the largest and best dwelling on earth; outside and in it is like pure gold; it is called Gladsheim. They built another hall that was the sanctuary of the goddesses, and it was a very beautiful building; it is called Vingolf.

There is, moreover, a great dwelling called Valaskjalf owned by Odin, which the gods built and roofed with pure silver. The high seat known as Hlidskjalf is there in this hall, and when All-father sits on this seat he sees over the whole world. In the southern end of heaven is the most beautiful hall of all, brighter than the sun; it is called Gimli; it shall stand when both heaven and earth have passed away, and good and righteous men will inhabit that place for all time.

Next they laid the hearth of a forge and then made hammer and tongs and an anvil, and thenceforward all other tools, and went on to work in metals and stone and wood, and also in gold, so abundantly that all their household utensils and furniture were of gold. That age was called the Golden Age before it was spoiled by the arrival of the women who came from Giantland.

Bifröst
From Heaven to Earth

The gods built a bridge from earth to heaven
called Bifröst. You will have seen it, but maybe
you call it the rainbow. It has three colours and
is very strong, and made with more skill and
cunning than other structures.

But strong as it is, it will break when the sons of Muspell ride out over it to harry, and their horses will swim over great rivers; and in this fashion they will come on the scene.

Bifröst is a good bridge, but there is nothing in this world that can be relied on when the sons of Muspell are on the war-path.

The red you see in the rainbow is flaming fire. If it were possible for all who wanted to go over Bifröst to do so, the frost ogres and cliff giants would scale heaven.

There are many beautiful places in heaven, and they are all under divine protection.

There is one called Alfheim, and there live the people called the light elves, but the dark elves live down in the earth and they are unlike the others in appearance and much more so in character. The light elves are fairer than the sun to look upon, but the dark elves, blacker than pitch.

Then there is Breidablik, there is no place more beautiful. There is also one called Glitnir, and its walls and posts and pillars are of red gold, but its roof is silver.

Further there is that place called Himinbjörg; it is at heaven's end by the bridge-head where Bifröst joins heaven.

It is said that there is another heaven to the south of and above this one, and there is yet a third heaven above these. At present, however, we think that it is inhabited only by white elves.

Yggdrasill
The World Tree

The chief place or sanctuary of the gods is by the ash Yggdrasill. There, every day, the gods have to hold court.

The ash is the best and greatest of all trees; its branches spread out over the whole world and reach up over heaven.

The tree is held in position by three roots that spread far out; one is among the Æsir, the second among the frost ogres where once was Ginnungagap, and the third extends over Niflheim.

Under the root that turns in the direction of the frost ogres lies the fountain of Mimir, in which is hidden wisdom and understanding; Mimir is the name of the owner of the fountain. He is full of wisdom because he drinks water from the fountain out of the horn Gjöl. All-father came there and asked for a single drink from the fountain, but he did not get it until he had given one of his eyes as a pledge. As it says in the Sybil's Vision:

> I know for certain Odin
> where you concealed your eye,
> in the famous
> fountain of Mimir;
> mead he drinks
> every morning
> from the pledge of the Father-of-the-slain.
> Do you know any more or not?

The third root of the ash tree is in the sky, and under that root is the very sacred fountain called the Fountain of Urd. There the gods hold their court of justice. The Æsir ride up to that place every day over the bridge Bifröst, which is also known as the bridge of the Æsir.

The Norns of Fate

There is a beautiful hall near the fountain under the ash tree, and from it come three maidens whose names are Urd, Verdandi, Skuld. These maidens shape the lives of men, and we call them Norns. There are, however, more Norns, those that come to every child that is born in order to shape its life, and these are beneficent, others belong to the family of the elves and a third group belongs to the family of dwarfs, as it says here:

> Of different origins
> are the Norns I think,
> not all of one kindred;
> some come from Æsir-kin,
> some from the elves
> and some are the daughters of Dvalin.

The Norns decide the fates of men, they appoint very unequal destinies for them; for some have a good and abundant life, but others have little wealth or fame. Some have a long life and others a short one. The good Norns who come from good stock shape good lives, but those who meet with misfortune owe it to the evil Norns.

It is said further that the Norns who live near the fountain of Urd draw water from the fountain every day, and along with it the clay that lies round about the fountain, and they besprinkle the ash so that its branches shall not wither or decay.

Life in Valhalla

All the men who have fallen in battle since the beginning of the world have now come to Odin in Valhalla. There is a huge crowd there, and there will be many more still, and yet they will seem too few when the wolf comes.

But there is never so big a crowd in Valhalla that they don't get enough pork from the boar called Sæhrimnir. He is boiled every day, and comes alive every evening.

Odin gives what food is on his table to two wolves, but he himself needs nothing to eat. Wine is for him both food and drink. Two ravens sit on his shoulders and bring to his ears all the news that they see or hear. He sends them out at daybreak to fly over the whole world, and they come back at breakfast-time; by this means he comes to know a great deal about what is going on, and on account of this men call him the god-of-ravens.

Every day after they have dressed, Odin's Champions put on their armour and go out into the courtyard and fight and lay one another low. That is their play and, when it is breakfast-time, they ride to the hall and sit down to drink.

There are, moreover, others whose duty it is to serve in Valhalla, carry the drink round and look after the table service and ale cups. These are called Valkyries. Odin sends them to every battle, and they choose death for the men destined to die, and award victory.

IV. Divine Treasures

The Wager

Once, for a joke, Loki cut off all Sif's hair, but
when Thor got to know this he seized Loki and
would have broken every bone in his body, had
he not sworn to persuade the dark elves to make
hair from gold for Sif that would grow like other
hair. After that Loki went to the dwarfs called
the sons of Ivaldi, and they made the hair,

Skidbladnir and the spear that Odin had, which is called Gungnir. Then Loki wagered his head with a dwarf called Brokk that his brother Eitri would not be able to make three other treasures as fine as these.

When they came to the smithy, Eitri laid a pig-skin in the furnace and told his brother Brokk to work the bellows and not to stop until he had taken what he had put there out of the forge. No sooner had he left the smithy than a fly settled on Brokk's hand and stung him, as he was working the bellows, but he kept them going as before, until the smith took the object from the forge – and there was a boar with bristles of gold.

Next he put gold in the furnace and told him to blow without stopping until he returned. He went away, and then the fly came and settled on Brokk's neck, stinging him twice as badly as before. He went on blowing, however, until the smith took from the forge the gold ring called Draupnir.

Then he put iron in the furnace and told him to blow, and said that everything would be spoiled if the bellows stopped working. This time the fly settled between his eyes and stung him on the eyelids so that the blood ran into his eyes and he could not see at all. He stopped the bellows and as quickly as possible brushed the fly away with one hand. At that moment the smith came in and said that everything in the furnace had been within an ace of being spoiled. Then he took from the forge a hammer and gave all the treasures to his brother Brokk, telling him to take them to Asgard to settle the wager.

Magic at Work

When Brokk and Loki brought out their
treasures, the Æsir sat down on their thrones
and the verdict given by Odin, Thor and Frey
was to stand good. Loki then gave Odin the
spear, Gungnir; Thor, the hair Sif was to have;
and Frey, Skidbladnir, and he explained what
sort of treasures they were: the spear never
missed its mark, the hair would grow to her
skin as soon as it was put on Sif's head, and
Skidbladnir got a breeze to take it where it had
to go as soon as its sail was hoisted, and it could
be folded together like a cloth and carried in

one's pouch, if so desired. Then Brokk produced
his treasures. He gave Odin the ring, saying that
every ninth night eight others as heavy as itself
would drop from it. To Frey he gave the boar,
saying that it could run through the air and over
the sea day or night faster than any horse, and
that no matter how gloomy it might be at night
or in the world of darkness, it would always be
brilliantly light where it was travelling; its bristles shone so. Then he gave the hammer to Thor
and said that he could hit anything that was
in his way with it as hard as he could and the
hammer would never break; and if he hurled it
at anything he would never loose it – no matter
how far it was flung it would return to his hand;
also, if he desired, it could become so small that
he could keep it in his shirt. It had, however,
one fault; it was rather short in the handle.

The Verdict

The decision of the gods was that the hammer was the most valuable of all the treasures and the best defence against the frost ogres, and they decided that the dwarf had won the wager. Then Loki offered to redeem his head but the dwarf said that he could not expect to do that. "Catch me, then!" said Loki, and when the dwarf tried to seize him he was already a long way off. Loki had shoes in which he could run through the air and over the sea. Then the dwarf asked Thor to catch him and he did so. The dwarf wanted to cut off his head, but Loki said he had a claim on his head but not his neck. The dwarf took a thong and a knife and tried to pierce holes in Loki's lips to sew them up, but the knife would not cut. Then he said that his brother's awl would be better and, as soon as he had mentioned it there it was, and it pierced the lips. He sewed up the mouth, and Loki tore the thong out through the holes.

A note on this edition

The Icelandic scholar and historian Snorri Sturluson (1179-1241) wrote the Edda or Prose Edda in about 1220. Written as a handbook for poets, it consists of four main parts: "Prologue," "The Deluding of Gylfi," "Poetic Diction" and "Account of Metres."

Most of the text in "The Viking Gods" is from "The Deluding of Gylfi," where King Gylfi converses with three knowledgeable beings known as High, Just-as-high, and Third. For the purpose of this book, this form has not been maintained.

In this edition, some of the material that Snorri covered in several places has been considerably condensed and rearranged into self-contained chapters. Snorri's original narrative order has also been changed in places.

Two fragments from "Poetic Diction," which are not included in Jean I. Young's translation, have been added to the accounts of the goddess Sif and the god Baldur for the purpose of continuity. Nothing has been added to Snorri's text, with the exception of two verses from one of his main sources, "The Sibyl's Vision" (Völuspá), at the end of the chapter The Creation of Man (translated by Bernard Scudder).

The complete text of Snorri Sturluson's "Deluding of Gylfi" is found in Jean I. Young's translation, together with part of the "Poetic Diction." A complete translation of the entire work has been made by Anthony Faulkes (Edda, published by Everyman's Library, 1987).

Snorri
Story-teller of the Gods

Snorri Sturluson was born in west Iceland in 1179 (possibly 1178), into one of the most powerful clans in Iceland, the Sturlungs. It was this family that eventually brought about the downfall of the old clan system, by continually striving to attain greater power and influence, and thereby disturbing the delicate balance among the six leading families on which society itself was based. Afterwards, when the whole of Iceland was embroiled in civil war, it proved easy for King Hákon of Norway to intercede, take control of the country and, in 1262, make it a Norwegian dependency.

Although Snorri was born into a position of wealth and power, providence ordained that culture and learning would also be a formative influence in his upbringing. As a boy he was sent to be fostered with the Oddi clan in south Iceland, which was the focal point of national learning at the time. Generations of the Oddi family had been educated on the continent, and this cultural environment, far more cosmopolitan than anywhere else in Iceland, was where the young Snorri was brought up and his personality undoubtedly shaped to a large extent.

Two separate and very clearly defined traits struggled for supremacy within Snorri's character: on the one hand a thirst for power and wealth, and on the other hand a keen spirit of inquiry and a vocation to become a writer. Throughout his life, Snorri worked systematically towards becoming one of the richest chieftains in Iceland, but at the same time he consistently devoted himself to literature and scholarship. The struggle for power brought about his downfall. Snorri had sided with Earl Skúli Bardarson against King Hákon of Norway, but once the king had gained the upper hand and had the earl killed, he took vengeance on Snorri by ordering a posse to attack and murder him at his farmstead in west Iceland, in 1241. By an ironic twist of fate, the King of Norway was instrumental in the murder of the very man who would immortalize the Norwegian monarchy, by recording its continuous history in literature of monumental stature.

Snorri's chief writings are the Heimskringla ("The Orb of the World"), a collection of Sagas tracing the unbroken history of the Kings of Norway from around AD400 to 1200; the Edda (Prose Edda or Snorra-Edda), on the Viking mythology; and also, in the opinion of the overwhelming majority of scholars, the Saga of Egill Skallagrímsson, one of the masterpieces of the Saga tradition. Of all the lives of the kings in the Heimskringla, the Saga of King Olaf the Holy deserves to be singled out for Snorri's brilliant story-telling and gift for structuring his material. There is no fundamental difference between Snorri's approach to history and sources and that of contemporary European historians, except that Snorri is largely distinguished by his faithfulness to his source material and his very conscious realist and objective avoidance of all exaggeration, interpretation and exegesis. His outstanding command of style makes the Saga of King Olaf, in my opinion, simply one of the best-written books in all world literature.

The Edda of Snorri Sturluson is by far the most impor-tant of all our sources about Viking lore and belief. It is also the only work directly attributed to Snorri; his name appears in the oldest manuscript, the Codex Upsaliensis, which is thought to have been copied just after 1300, a little more than half a century after the author's death. It is divided into four parts: Prologue, the Deluding of Gylfi, Poetic Diction and Account of Metres. Written in the same vein and style as other Icelandic works from this time, it is faithful to contemporary notions of the divine origin of monarchy, as Snorri traces the descent of the Kings of Sweden back to the gods. However, Snorri is unrivalled for the wealth of information he presents about the Vikings' ideas about the creation of the world and the deeds of the gods. Snorri's talent for bringing learning to life, and his combination of scholarly methods and entertaining story-telling, flourish into magnificent descriptions of the quali-ties and shortcomings of the Viking gods, told with both engagement and humour. The gods are characterized as human and fallible, yet never lose their essential dignity. On one level, the Edda is a handbook for poets; in his Poetic Diction, Snorri explains the complex mythological epithets and metaphors of the ancient poetry, while his Account of Metres is a compendium illustrating some 100 different classical metres.

Snorri Sturluson is a remarkable combination of the edu-cated scholar who is at home in European learning and contemporary tradition, and the writer for ordinary people who has a clear sense of the best way to tell entertaining stories. He makes the lives of the gods into something that is, quite simply, fun to read. His work is the product of extensive knowledge of ancient literary tradition and the unique combination of history and fiction that developed into medieval Icelandic literature. But although he was writing in Iceland, using Icelandic sources, his viewpoint is consistently international: he is fully aware that his subject is the common heritage of all Scandinavia and thereby Europe, and his work is an invaluable record of the way that the Vikings perceived life and the world about them.

Páll Valsson
Senior Lecturer in Icelandic, University of Uppsala, Sweden

Lorenz Frölich

Lorenz Frölich (1820-1908), was of a well-to-do
Copenhagen family with an international background. He
aspired to become a painter of historic subjects and after
having studied art in Denmark, he went to Germany in
1840 for further studies. From Germany he went to Italy
in 1846, where he stayed for five years, and after that he
went to Paris. In Paris he settled down and lived there and
worked from 1851 to 1875, only once staying for more
than a short period in Denmark.

His solemn wish to paint motifs from history came only
partly true. He became mainly an illustrator, famous for his
brilliant drawings. Among his best known works are illustrations of a poem by the Danish poet Oehlenschläger, com-
pleted in 1844, and illustrations of the History of Denmark
by Fabricius in 1852. Later followed a series of children's
books, which became quite popular, especially those about
his own daughter "Mlle. Lili." Frölich is, however, best
known as being one of the two supreme illustrators of H. C.
Andersen's fairy tales.

Of his other important work, mention must be made
of the series of etchings inspired by classical literature
("Amor et Psyché in 1862"), and of course "Thor and Loki
at Utgard" and "The Nordic Gods" (1874-83) based on
tales from the old Nordic mythology. In his illustrations he
recreates with his fertile imagination a long-gone world of
powerful men and strong-willed women. Here we encoun-
ter Frölich's broad epic talent, his sense of humour and his
flair for detail.

Later in his life (1895) Frölich illustrated the Elder Edda
in K. Gjellerup's Danish translation. These are line drawings, which duly respect the dimensions of the page, and do
not try to create an atmosphere by an ornate style. Almost
sparingly drawn figures of personae and the accompanying
words say it all.

Seldom did the opportunity arise for Frölich to paint old
Nordic motifs in large format. The most important of these
are "Thor in his Chariot" and "The Death of Baldur," both
painted in the period of 1853-57 for a mansion in South
Jutland. These paintings are now to be found at Snoghöj
Academy. When Fredriksborg Palace was rebuilt he painted

"Gefion Ploughs Sjælland" (1882). None of these paintings possesses, however, the intense atmosphere found in the drawings of the Nordic gods and the Edda.

Hanne Westergaard
Former curator, Department of Painting and Sculpture, The Royal Museum of Fine Arts, Copenhagen.

Index of Names

Fountain of Urd, under the roots of Yggdrasill, where the gods hold their court of Justice

Frey, god of fertility, son of Njörd

Freyja, goddess of love, daughter of Njörd, wife of Od

Frigg, foremost of the goddesses, wife of Odin, mother of Baldur

Garm, a monster dog, battles with Tyr at Ragnarök

Giantland, home of the frost ogres and cliff giants

Gimli (Shelter-from-fire), the most beautiful hall in heaven, the best place to be after Ragnarök

Ginnungagap, the great void between Muspell and Niflheim

Gjöll, Heimdall's trumpet, its blast can be heard all over the world

Gladsheim (Radiant-home), a temple in Asgard, a meeting-place for Odin and the twelve gods.

Gleipnir, the fetter that the Fenriswolf could not break, made from the noise a cat makes when it moves, the beard of a woman, the roots of a mountain, the sinews of a bear, the breath of a fish and the spittle of a bird

Glitnir, Forseti's hall. It is made with pillars of gold and roofed with silver

Gnipa Cave, by the entrance to Niflheim, dwelling of the dog Garm

Goldtooth, a name for Heimdall, who had teeth of gold

Goldtuft, Heimdall's horse

Grimnir, a name for Odin

Gungnir, Odin's spear that never misses its mark

Heimdall, warden of the gods

Hel, daughter of Loki, presides over the ninth world in Niflheim

Himinbjörg (Cliffs-of-heaven), Heimdall's dwelling by Bifröst

Hlidskjalf, Odin's throne, from where he could see over the whole world

Höd, the blind god, killer of Baldur the Good

Hringhorni, Baldur's ship

Idavöll, in the centre of Asgard

Idun, keeper of the apples of youth, wife of Bragi

Ivaldi, father to some dwarfs who made Skidbladnir, Frey's ship

Kvasir, a man made by the gods from spit

Loki, the mischiefmonger of the Æsir, son of a giant, father of the Midgard Serpent, the wolf Fenrir and Hel

Midgard serpent, one of Loki's children. It lies in the middle of the ocean round the earth, biting its own tail

Midgard, a stronghold built by the gods and given to men to live in. Its walls are built of Ymir's eyebrows

Mimir, owner of the fountain of wisdom and understanding beside Yggdrasill

Mjölnir, Thor's hammer

Muspell, the first world to exist

Nanna, wife of Baldur

Narvi, son of Loki and Sigyn

Nastrand (Shore-of-death), the place where murderers and perjurers will dwell after Ragnarök.

Necklace of the Brisings, Freyja's necklace, believed to have magical properties

Niflheim, the ninth world

Njörd, god of wind, sea and fire. To be called on for wealth and prosperity. Husband of Skadi. Father of Frey and Freyja

Noatun, the hall of Njörd in Asgard

Od, husband of Freyja

Odin, All-father, Valfather. The oldest and most important of the gods

Ragnarök, the final battle where all the forces of evil fight against the gods

Rind, mother of Vali

Sessrumnir (With-many-seats), Freyja's hall in heaven

Sif, wife of Thor

Sigyn, Loki's wife, mother of Narvi

Skadi, goddess of skiing and hunting, daughter of the giant Thjazi, wife of Njördur

Skidbladnir, Frey's ship

Skuld, one of the three Norns by the Fountain of Fate

Surt, a giant guarding Muspell

Sæhrimnir, a boar in Valhalla which the Champions feed on, it is boiled every day and comes alive every night

Thjazi, a giant, father of Skadi

Thor, god of thunder, the foremost of the gods after Odin his father

Thrudvangar (Plains-of-power), Thor's realm in Asgard

Thrymheim (Storm-home), Thjazi's homestead, where his daughter Skadi made her home after his death

Tyr, the one-handed god of the brave, son of Frigg

Ull, god of hunting and skiing, son of Sif

Urd, one of the three Norns by the Fountain of Fate

Vaifather (Father-of-the-slain), one of Odin's many names

Valaskjalf, Odin's dwelling in Asgard. It is built and roofed with pure silver

Valhalla (Hall-of-the-slain), Odin's hall in Asgard where all who die in battle gather

Vali, god of battles and marksmanship, son of Odin

Valkyries, Odin's maidens, who serve in Valhalla and go to battles where they choose death or victory for men

Vanheim, the realm in which the people of the Vanir live

Ve, son of Bor and Bestla

Verdandi, one of the three Norns by the Fountain of Fate

Vidar, the silent god, almost as strong as Thor, kills the wolf Fenrir at Ragnarök

Vili, son of Bor and Bestla

Vingolf, sanctuary of the goddesses in Asgard

Yggdrasill, the world tree in the centre of the universe

Ymir, the first living creature, a giant. Ancestor of all the evil race of giants

Æsir, the gods